The Star

Images of
Doncaster

The **Star**

Images of
Doncaster

The Breedon Books
Publishing Company
Derby

First published in Great Britain by
The Breedon Books Publishing Company Limited
44 Friar Gate, Derby, DE1 1DA
1995

The Author

ALAN BERRY, who has written the captions for the photographs in *Images of Doncaster,* was born in the town in 1929.

An old Danensian, he started his newspaper career as a junior reporter on the former *Doncaster Chronicle* and *Yorkshire Evening Post* when he was 16.

He was subsequently a member of the editorial staffs of the *Yorkshire Evening News,* the *Doncaster Gazette,* the *Doncaster Evening Post* (where he was deputy editor) and latterly *The Star* as feature writer.

He was appointed MBE for services to journalism in 1990.

ISBN 1 85983 037 4

Printed and bound by Butler & Tanner, Frome, Somerset.
Jackets printed by Premier Print, Nottingham.
Colour separations by Colour Services, Leicester.

Contents

Bygone Days 6

Old Buildings 35

Public Houses 43

Town of Trade 50

Entertainment 56

Royal Visits 62

Transport 68

Horse Racing 86

Street Scenes 94

Down the Pit 100

The Miners' Strike of 1984 115

Industry 120

Churches 121

Going to War 124

Civic Affairs 129

Telling the News 130

Healing the Sick 132

Doncaster from the Air 133

Wadworth 140

Thorne .141

Tickhill 146

Sprotborough 148

Conisbrough 152

Sporting Days 158

Schooldays 167

Stormy Weather 169

Subscribers 173

Bygone Days

The young madame fourth from the left, middle row, will SEE ME AFTER SCHOOL! Tongue out at the nice cameraman indeed! Sir (believed to be Mr Goodhead) and 27 of the infants at Askern Council School and not a smile on any of them.

First Small Boy: "What about it, then, are yer gonner join up?"

Second Small Boy (hands in his empty pocket): "Nah! Tha knaws ah'm skint reight enough but all yer gets is t' Queen's shillin' onyroad."

F.S.M.: "Good uniform, though, innit!".

S.S.M.: "Daft sort of 'at. And all ah can play is t'pianner. Imagine going ter battle playing t' pianner."

Young Doncaster takes a critical look at the bandsmen of the Yorkshire Dragoons camped at Doncaster. The picture is undated.

Edgar Scrivens photographed everything, everywhere. Here he snaps an early example of drag – a collector with 'her' box in 'her' basket. The 'farmer's boy' also has a box. The occasion was the annual fund-raising Doncaster Infirmary Sunday parade.

That's the Mayor on a tank, and that's the Vicar ...or is it the Archdeacon? And there's Egbert the Tank. Daft name for a tank. This postcard is described as illustrating Tank Bank Week. In the background, Doncaster Corn Exchange.

Photographers didn't much mind disasters – fires, trams off the rails, steam engines in trouble, raging floods. They could turn their pictures into postcards and make a penny or two. That's what E.L.Scrivens did with this gaunt masterpiece entitled 'Fire at Woodhouse and Co's Brass Works, September 23, 1908.' The factory was at Hexthorpe. On the back it does NOT say "Having a lovely time at Hexthorpe, wish you were here."

WE see 'Cleeth' on one deckchair and 'thorpes' on another so we know which beach. But which Doncaster club outing (if that is what it is) is not stated. Can't have been a very nice day, everyone is fully clothed in hats, scarves, ties, coats, suits. Couple of alluring good-lookers languishing sleepily in the middle, but Ma has them well chaperoned, to be sure.

'Garden fête, Hatfield Vicarage.' You don't sit at garden fêtes, see. You stands, talks nicely, buys stuff you don't want at stalls. The smart set at St Lawrence's enjoy tea served by the ladies of the parish.

Decorated bicycles, fancy dress. The place is Hatfield, the time and occasion not recorded on the picture.

Not a saboteur in sight when the Hunt met at Tickhill Spital at the crossroads between Tickhill and Bawtry.

All properly starched, and everything whiter than white when the workers posed for this one outside Balby Road laundry.

Doing all right is our chimney sweep. Doesn't use his old push-barrow any more; got himself a little Ford car now. Mr Mason, popular Doncaster photographer, who used to have a place in Bower's Fold, took the picture.

Under the spreading (chestnut?) tree the village smithy stands at Epworth. The smith, a mighty man, was also wheelwright it seems, because there is an iron tyre leaning on the smithy door and a cart wheel awaiting repair.

Ramsay MacDonald formed the second Labour government in 1929 and here he is with Lord Arnold and Tom Williams, third from right. It's unmistakeably Tom Williams because he always wore wing collars. Mr Williams, the Member for Don Valley, had an unassailable majority – one of the largest in the country – at any election. He was extremely popular and often described in the post-war years as 'the best Minister of Agriculture we ever had'. He held the post from 1945-51.

The Rt Hon Tom was deservedly to become Lord Williams of Barnburgh (where he had once been a colliery checkweighman). He lived in Town Moor Avenue, Doncaster, in his later years.

Toby waits patiently on the Punch and Judy. There's a piano for an open-air sing-song, there's a big tea urn at the end of the table, and we're all set to tuck in because this is the Ashmount Club, Balby, children's outing 80 years ago.

An entire battalion of the King's Own Yorkshire Light Infantry came to Cusworth Hall, home of the Battie-Wrightson family after Lady Isabella Battie-Wrightson bought her son Robert Cecil a commission in the regiment. She is seen with him (the young man holding the sword, fourth right). This is only part of a larger picture of the full Battalion.

Doncaster Parish Church, with the old Vicarage, and a Humber keel of 'Sheffield Size' on the South Yorkshire Navigation. Keels had square sails and worked the rivers and canals throughout Yorkshire. Keelmen and thei families, although based in villages like Stainforth an Thorne, lived in a tiny cabin in the stern (note mother an

baby on this one). When there was no wind mother frequently walked the towpath dragging the boat while her husband steered it.

You can see a working keelboat today – the late skipper Fred Schofield's Comrade, owned by the Humber Keel and Sloop Preservation Society, is moored at South Ferriby.

Foggy day in Ellerker Avenue, Hexthorpe, J.Berry's shop at the corner. Can't think of any good reason why anyone should want to waste film on this one, but the adverts are interesting. Above, left to right: It's an Odd House Where There's No Oxo; Players Digger tobaccos; Diphtheria Kills; Civil Defence. Below: Grand Theatre; Essoldo Cinema showing *Sierra* and Norman Evans and Jimmy James in *Over the Garden Wall*; Don't Waste Fuel; something illegible; and For a Man's Life with Good Pay Join the Regular Army. Good old days, eh!

Wheatley Junior Mixed School, Beckett Road, class of '48. What a lot of nice happy-looking kids!

The Old Mill – replaced by St Mary's Bridge. This is where you came if you wanted to see just how high the river was after torrential rain. This is where you came to watch the swirling (and often stinking) frothing waters and wonder how long it would be before the bank burst somewhere, and Bentley or Arksey or Sprotbrough would be inundated. This is where I was dragged by my mother after severe whooping cough. 'Walk him up and down the towpath, Mrs Berry' said Dr Evans. 'Let him sniff the fumes!' Must have worked. We both lived long after to tell the tale!

"The rest of you get on with your work. You, Billy, you come stand next to me." That's what Miss MIGHT have said, but it is doubtful if any of the children could hear her. This is a class of deaf youngsters and 'Miss' skilfully demonstrates, in her beautiful handwriting, how to join up the letters.

The world-famous Yorkshire Institution for the Deaf and Dumb, or later called Yorkshire Residential School for the Deaf in Leger Way, Doncaster owes its origin to the Rev William Carr Fenton, one-time vicar of Mattersey, near Bawtry. The school opened in the former Eastfield House, near Doncaster Racecourse in 1829. On the wall of our 1905 picture, an abacus; on the table a cricket bat and toy cart.

Oh, Mr Porter what have we here? The Coronation of King Edward in 1902 was a good opportunity for a little advertising by local shopkeepers. The parade of floats moves north along High Street, passing Hepworth's printers and stationers, and Parkinson's Café, with Porter's float in the vanguard. A Mr Porter sold pots; perhaps it is he?

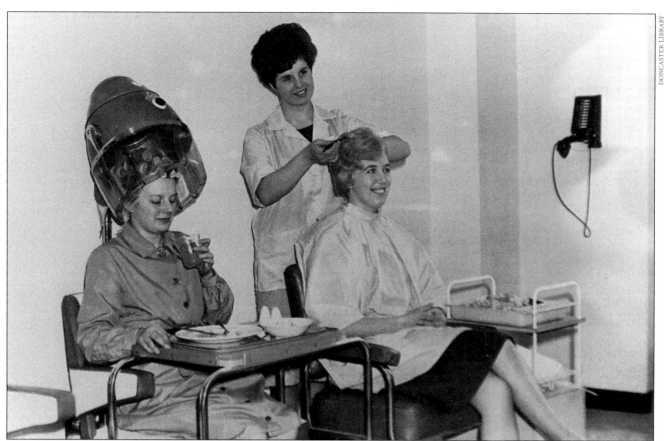

You can have your hair done at work when you're an employee of Marks & Spencer – and you can have your dinner and a glass of orange juice while under the drier, which all saves time to do a bit of lunchtime shopping. doesn't it! (At M & S, we should hope!) In-house hairdressing was a novelty at the Doncaster branch in 1965. Janet Griffiths is the stylist.

Just look at the size of those loaves! Big enough to feed a family of ten. Which is probably what they had to do, because our picture of a soup kitchen, taken in Tickhill a hundred years ago, is entitled 'Tickhill Relief Distribution'. The people were hungry because of the bad weather, so two ladies set about relieving their distress. But we are bound to say they all look plump and cheerful in this picture; maybe they are all givers, not receivers.

The men wear what appear to be berets, or Tam O'Shanters, but we are in deepest South Yorkshire, not France or Scotland. This is the Conisbrough Fire Brigade with the shield they won at hydrant drill. The 'engine' is horse-drawn; the date about 1900.

Traffic in Prospect Place was down to two pedal cars and our kid's new bike for the Jubilee of King George and Queen Mary in 1935. Had real cars ventured here, they would have been limited to 30mph – 1935 was the year of Mr Belisha's pedestrian crossings and the imposition of a speed restriction in built-up places like Prospect Place. The street was between Cemetery Road and Upper Oxford Street.

We don't know who they were, but they look happy, their dresses could still be fashionable today, and they've all had their hair bobbed because you want to look nice for the street party. The occasion is the Coronation of King George VI in 1937 and it says Long Live the King over the front door of this house in Park Terrace, in the centre of Doncaster. If the kerbstones look strange it's because they'd coloured them red, white and blue.

Coal House, the NCB headquarters, rises in the background; the church of St John the Apostle, a daughter church to Christ Church, is still there in Catherine Street, the County Court building with its rare Edward VIII armorial is on the left. The date is 1965. Now in the 1990s Coal House still stands, so does the court building greatly modernised, but much of the rest has vanished.

Every few months in the 1960s and 70s local newspapers like the *Doncaster Evening Post*, the *Gazette*, and *The Star* reported under the general heading 'The changing face of Doncaster'. This illustrated one of those features. On the right is the Southern bus station in its early stages. On the left is Spring Gardens Methodist church, originally part of the Primitive Methodist tradition... in its final stages.

Tony Barber – Lord Barber – whose boyhood was spent in Doncaster and who went to school at Retford, became MP for Doncaster and was chancellor throughout Edward Heath's premiership 1970-74. Here he poses for the traditional picture en route to the House to present his budget in 1971.

'Doncaster cattle market swings back into action' was the caption to this Sheffield Newspapers photograph in the 1980s. But not for long. The livestock market closed and for a time the building was used – rather imaginatively – by local college drama students as an admirable forum-cum-amphitheatre in which to stage plays.

One of the most impressive buildings in Tickhill is that containing the Parish Rooms in Northgate, easily missed by a careful motorist approaching the junction with Sunderland Street. It was originally St Leonards hospital, founded in 1225, but the present black and white façade dates from the fifteenth century. The building has been a police station, and a school. The Women's Institute hold a weekly produce market here – and there is always a queue for the homemade cakes, pies, quiches and preserves.

The Dell Café, Hexthorpe Flatts. Here's a picture to bring back memories of sunny pram-pushing summers, afternoon tea, ice creams, then a stroll around the thatched bandstand on an island at the bottom of the famous sunken gardens. The café was built in 1928.

The old Manor House, Hexthorpe. An account by a Doncaster historian written in the early nineteenth century says the manor of Hexthorpe has a history going back to the time of Edward the Confessor. In fact, Hexthorpe may at one time have been a more important place than Doncaster Borough, with which it merged in 1914. This picture was taken in 1984.

Now, in the 1990s, it takes perhaps a couple of men and some mighty machinery and in a day or two all is safely gathered in. But then it was a field full of folk, raw cut hands and sore knees, and weeks of back-breaking work. The women are scrattin' for taters at Arksey in 1946. A plough and perhaps a spinner dislodged the spud when I first joined the wartime spud pickers (like we see here.) They still had to be gathered first into baskets, then into carts, to be taken to the potato pie near the field gate.

COLLECTION OF BENTLEY WITH ARKSEY HERITAGE SOCIETY

It might be any village green, anywhere in deepest rural England, but the venue is instantly recognisable by anyone who knows Woodlands. Occasion is that colourful traditional religious event, a Whit Sing, lead by robed choristers. The piano is on a horse-drawn wagon.

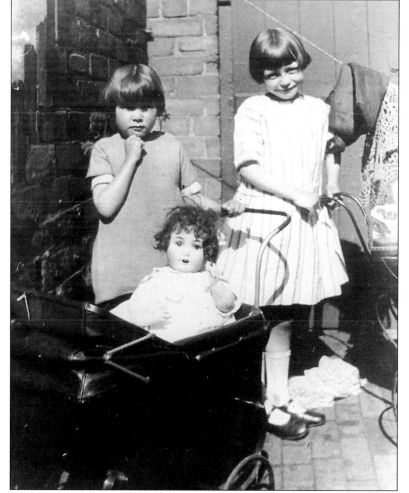

Mrs E.Hill was happy to let us publish this one. The scene is a back yard in Palmer Street, Hyde Park, and they're playing the game of which children never seemed to tire: Being Grown-Ups. Perhaps the two charmers are now very grown up indeed, and pushing their grandchildren's prams today. There is no date but hair and shoe styles suggest it was over 50 years ago.

It was bad, but not a terminal disaster. The Crompton Parkinson factory in Wheatley caught fire in June 1988 and *Doncaster Star* photographer Steve Taylor arrived at the height of the blaze.

When this picture was taken in 1968 Barnburgh St Mary's was threatened by mining subsidence, and the children were all set to do a ten-mile sponsored walk to raise money for its restoration. Barnburgh, says the Official Guide, is known as the Cat and Man Town following the story of Sir Percival Cresacre who is said to have killed a wild cat in the church porch, but died of wounds inflicted by the animal. 'Cat Kills Man!' – sounds like the proverbial man bites dog 'good story' sought by all journalists but there weren't many around in 1477. The clergyman is the then Vicar, the Rev W.J.Parker.

MR GEORGE ROPER

"Dyb Dyb Dyb!" said the Scoutmaster. And "We'll Dob Dob Dob!" we would reply. Do Your Best, We'll Do Our Best ... Remember? Here the Rev Mr Challis is seen with the 15th St Jude's Own Scouts at Hexthorpe in the 'bad old days' of 1926. Not so bad, however, when you could muster a troop as smart as this. Look: Everyone's got bare knees except the parson. And look again: They wear the sort of hats the great chief Baden-Powell always wore. The picture, bursting with proper pride and achievement, has something to teach us today..

THE YORKSHIRE POST

Picture Editor to photographer: "It's a 36-page paper on Friday and it's not all advertising so we want lots more pictures. I've seen your diary. You've got ten minutes doing nothing between that wedding at Carcroft and that presentation at Thorne. So get out there, anywhere, and bring us back some good pics."

How a crisis concentrates the mind! Photographer uses a few short well-known journalistic phrases, gulps rest of hot coffee, grabs camera box and rolls of film, leaps into battered Ford Popular, scours town especially council parks, and that's how great pictures like this are made. (I know; I was picture editor.) Every expression here speaks volumes. We think the boys, seen outside the Wheatley branch library, are from the Park School next door. Where are they now, we wonder..

MISS K BRAMWITH

A reporter looking for local colour in the days of the Blitz in the 1940s, but not wishing to give away any military secrets, discovered, to his amazement, an ARP Post in what had been the old men's shelter in leafy Hexthorpe Flatts. Picture, if you can, the tension, the drama, the red alerts, the smelly gasmasks... the endless games of darts. Sandbagged and secluded, he found the wardens were ready for anything the Nazi war machine might throw at them. Now see here the stirrup pumps, the gas rattles, the tin hats, the gas capes, the fire buckets, the handbells and our young 'un front row, right.

And first you must eat some lovely plain bread and butter! That's what Our Mam said. Just dying to grab a cream cake are these patient youngsters photographed before the feast at the Oxford Place Peace celebrations in July 1919. The picture comes courtesy of Mrs Joan Warnock, and that's Joan at the end of the table, front left (with a ribbon in her hair.) Oxford Place, with its blackened stone Italian-style Wesleyan chapel and school, was a delightful cul-de-sac of some 40 houses and cottages off St James Street. All demolished now, of course.

Another peace celebration in 1919 – this time in Edlington. Floats, Union flags, and a lad on a decorated tricycle. Derek Porter let us use the picture.

Old Buildings

The interior of Doncaster Corn Exchange, date unknown. The occasion appears to be a flower fruit and veg show, or perhaps a chrysanthemum society annual competition. The top-hatted attendant keeps guard in case any of those young varmints pinches the flowers! The building dates from 1873 and has been used for concerts, choir festivals, brass band contests, political rallies, church bazaars, a British or Municipal Restaurant, boxing shows, all-in wrestling. Just about every major public event was held in Doncaster Corn Exchange for a hundred years. And yes, in the early days it was a public corn market.

Many of the great artistes of the past century have sung or played in this magnificent building, a monument to Victorian solidarity and certainty, which could seat 1,600 under a magnificent wrought-iron roof. More recently the space in the photograph was filled with stalls selling bed linen, towels, paperbacks, records, wallpaper, pet products and so on – not the purpose for which it was intended.

Note the small plaques in front of the balconies between the pillars. Each bore the name of a famous composer. Fire caused £1m damage in 1994, and there are plans to restore the area for cultural activities as well as trade.

Another view of Doncaster Corn Exchange before the alterations were made to the foreground stalls space. The sculpture above the entrance is well worth a moment's attention before you select your pound of sprouts and bunch of rhubarb.

Nether Hall when it was the offices of the Doncaster Rural District Council. The building, originally a private residence of the Copley family, had been central to a large estate called Nether Hall Park, which extended as far as the banks of the River Don to the north and Thorne Road to the south. Nether Hall is now used as a finance department by Doncaster MBC. The stained glass in the entrance hall is good value.

This is Beechfield House, which was in Waterdale. We look at the south side of the building, facing the park. Beechfield was the private residence of the Morris family until bought by Doncaster Corporation in 1907, and became both a museum and art gallery. The house was demolished in the early 1960s and Doncaster College, police HQ and court buildings, and car park occupy the site. These windows looked out on flower beds, lawns, sunken paths and secluded arbours. Half Doncaster did its courting there.

And there was an astonishing heated grotto, a man-made cavern plunging deep beneath the gardens. You pushed open a little green door and you descended on wet, mossy steps into a tropical rainforest! Behind one of these windows in our picture was a glass-fronted beehive, the bees passing in and out via a tube to the window ledge, all safely observed by visitors.

And what child now grown to grandparent can ever forget the Samurai warrior, lurking in a dark recess, bristling with ferocity? You came upon him suddenly. It was the first time you felt fear!

Bawtry Hall, now a centre of religious and charitable activity, recently the HQ of No.1 Bomber Command, RAF, was the home of the Peake family and this picture appears to have been taken around that time when they were in residence.

Among the attractions for the visitor then was the lake – made available to all the local children when frozen over for ice skating. It was also the traditional venue for the Whit Monday garden fête, and a nativity play in the coach house. The site may originally have been a Roman fort. There are still some fine trees and rhododendron bushes here. Modern houses continue to fill the surrounding park.

The posh name was The Subscription Rooms – but this building with its Ionic columns and classical façade was what we would today call a betting shop or a casino! Here, nearly 160 years ago, came the gentry and nobility of the pleasant country town of Doncaster to read the papers, write their letters and have a bet – at the tables or on a horse. 'Subscription' comes from the system whereby the punters each paid one guinea subscription to be Members.

"Just popping along to the Subscription Rooms, darling!" Sounds quite respectable! Victorian hostility to gambling, chiefly from Doncaster clergymen who hated Raceweek in particular, caused its demise as betting rooms and only the front remains. In recent times the building was a furniture shop and passers-by, unaware of its history, were astonished to discover, when the premises were vacated, that such an attractive building had been there all the time. The façade is now happily preserved.

'Sandy' Senior sits with obvious satisfaction outside his Sand House, cut out of the living sandstone between what was Green Dyke Lane and Balby Road. New houses, high-rise flats, and roads fill the space today. Sandy and family were sand merchants who carved their home straight out of their workplace. The project became more ambitious as the work progressed and soon the family had a kind of 'folly' on their hands. Everything was cut from the rock – four bedrooms, bathroom, stairs, stables, even a ballroom.

Sandy filled the house with huge carvings (a full-size elephant was memorable). In later years it was one of the wonders of Doncaster; you walked up by the side of the Alma Inn and you paid a shilling to look round what was in fact a warm, well-furnished residence

Another view of the creeper-clad Sand House. The building was 120ft long, the walls between a yard and three yards thick. A tiled roof kept the rain off. If the Sand House had not fallen into decay, or been destroyed to satisfy the need for new homes and roads, it would have been a huge tourist attraction today.

Wheatley Hall, former home of the Cooke family. They sold up in 1924 and moved south. The hall, which was close to the River Don, was pulled down in 1938 and factories occupy the site today.

The scene is Duke Street and Colonnades shopping and office precinct, above a car park, under construction. The date is 1983.

Doncaster Guildhall or Town Hall in Frenchgate was demolished in the 1960s and Marks & Spencers were among stores which replaced it. It was a magnificent and unforgettable building with imposing smoke-blackened columns, designed by John Butterfield in 1847. On the top was a figure of Justice (whose head was rescued by the demolition men). In its final years it housed the Borough Police, and the Borough Magistrates' courts were behind in a separate building of 1881. You reached the court entrance down a suitably gloomy alleyway to the left of the Guildhall. There were 24 cells below ground, prisoners coming up through a stairway right into the dock in the centre of the court. Our pictures show the Guildhall frontage, demolition work on the courthouse behind it, and Justice rather worse for wear.

Public Houses

Where traffic roars today was once this peaceful haven of Summer sunshine and shadow. The old gentleman nods off, the little girl turns and looks at the man with the funny camera, and a busy housewife drags her shopping home. In the background is St George Gate, and all except the graveyard of St George's Church, behind the railings, was swept away for the Doncaster ring road. And the world is an uglier place for it.

The Waverley Hotel, the snug White Lion (remember you walked down the side to the back bar?), the old Public Library, Reference Library, Beetham's pub with the heavy iron fender, a trial of strength for young men.

And Swaby's gents' hairdressers (a biscuit for every good boy), those Georgian front door steps with foot scrapers leading to solicitors' offices, Garrison Deakin the studio photographers? The piano teacher's studio – she who advertised that she had been a pupil of the great French pianist Alfred Cortot, an authority on Chopin?
All gone, gone, gone.

The Earl of Doncaster Arms Hotel offered 'good stabling' when this photograph was taken. If you preferred something faster, you could buy a motorcycle or small car next door. This is Bennetthorpe (or Bennitthorpe), west side, and a modern 'Earl' built before World War Two replaces the old hotel. The later garage on this site, and the one most will remember was that of Edgar Charlesworth, the main Ford dealer, who became widely respected for his work with National Savings, but even this has now disappeared to be replaced by a computer-age office block. The New Trent Brewery at Crowle, advertised on the garage wall is also no more.

The Rockingham Inn when William White was able to offer 'good stabling' just like the Earl of Doncaster, almost opposite, in Bennetthorpe. There's a newer, grander Rockingham today. A hundred years ago the Rockingham catered not only for the thirsty traveller and punter *en route* to the races, but for other thirsty sportsmen – Belle Vue Cricket and Football Grounds were close by. A Mr Bennett is said to have given his name to this finest of the approaches to Doncaster. He lived in a cottage here.

Eyes right, brakes on, there's a photographer taking my picture! The Crown Inn at Harlington, north of Doncaster, thirty years ago.

So this is Old George, is it! Down to his last bit of candle! The public house with its attractive iron flower boxes stands at the entrance to the once-narrow alley from Silver Street known as Bower's Fold (sometime called Boar's Fold). It is one of many welcoming hostelries which look on to the Market Place. Our picture was taken in 1984.

It was The Green House Hotel when this picture was taken in 1984 (later the Cumberland Hotel). Those Jacobean-style windows give it great elegance. A farmhouse when my orphaned Uncle Reg was live-in farm boy, it was probably once a post house, and is said to have been the HQ of General Wade when an army of about 6,000 troops was camped here at the time of the Rebellion of '45. There used to be a picture of Alderman Tuby, the town's Victorian showman-mayor, in the lounge. Whatever happened to it? Love the chimneys...

The Horse and Groom on the
road from Armthorpe to Cantley.
It's the television era, middle
1970s (note the aerial) but did
people really enjoy their pint of
John Smith's sitting so close to
traffic on this busy road?

Lovely windows, fine
proportions... the Waverley Hotel
in St George Gate after that street
was cut across by the Doncaster
Ring Road. It dwarfs the White
Lion (Barnsley Bitter,
remember?) and seems to have
catered largely for commercials
('reps' today). Its days were
numbered when this picture was
taken. Littlewoods store is on the
site.

The Bee Hive Hotel, another of John Smith's pubs, in the centre of Doncaster, photographed by the man from Doncaster Newspapers in 1970.

The Salutation and Cavalier Restaurant photographed in 1984. The façade, jealously preserved over the last 187 years, remains very much as it always has been. 'The Sal' must be one of very few public houses in South Yorkshire to merit a booklet of its own. Peter Coote's well-researched work (his father was landlord for 20 years) was published by Doncaster Civic Trust in 1991 and may still be bought in Doncaster. This is actually the 'new' Salutation; the first is recorded in the 1740s.

The brewer as patron of the arts. Craftsmanship and design combine at the Nag's Head Hotel, St Sepulchre Gate. Shoppers rushing to and fro beneath ought to stand and stare now and then – Doncaster streets have a wealth of interest at this higher level.

This was the view from the top of a Bentley bus as it waited at the terminus on North Bridge – the Volunteer Inn, with St George's Church in the background. The place had something of a reputation for prize fighting, and the walls were covered with pictures of bare-fisted pugilists facing up to each other long ago. The photograph is dated 1961.

Parents and children gather outside the White Hart Inn at Wadworth holding traditional floral decorations for the Maypole. The date must be pre-World War One. The custom continues at Wadworth.

The Coach and Horses public house, Scot Lane before the street was widened and today's Coach and Horses was built. It was Shipstones then and remained so for many years.

The Druids Arms at Bentley when Arthur Marshall had it. You'll not remember Arthur (the picture was taken 90 years ago) but that's probably him with the watch, and that's likely his missus, and it's probably his lad on the left with the hoop in his hand. Whitworth Son & Nephew brewed their 'famous Doncaster ales' as advertised here at premises in Cleveland Street. Today's Druids is on the same site, but an entirely different building.

Beer is Best and Balby Brewery Beer was best of all brews. Or so Frank Pickering, licensed brewer, pictured with his draymen, would have you believe. Pickering's Brewery was in Back Lane (Sandford Road) and was one of a dozen independent outfits listed in Doncaster and district early this century. Two firms were described as Botanical Brewers – were these Dandelion and Burdock men or Herb Beer makers? Botanical Brewers indeed!

Town of Trade

Ecstasy! When the Arndale Centre was built in St Sepulchre Gate/Frenchgate, replacing all those old premises like the Angel and Royal Hotel, Hodgson and Hepworths, Davy's shop and café 'rad and so on, this statue appeared in the main mall. The old ladies tut-tutted and thought it disgusting, the young found it interesting, and maybe it represented the times we lived in. But it didn't stay for long. When Arndale Centre became the Frenchgate Centre the young lovers were banished from this shopping Eden and were last seen, still in this ecstatic embrace, in a suburban garden.

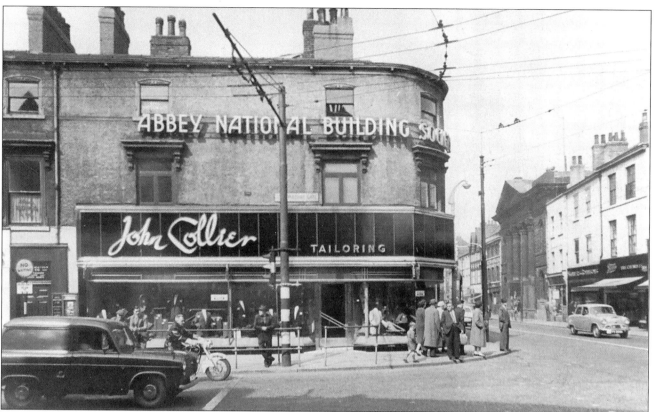

St Sepulchre Gate in the foreground, Frenchgate to the right in the days before the Arndale Centre, before pedestrianisation, and before motorcyclists were made to wear crash helmets. The building with the stone columns is the Guildhall Borough Police HQ.

Meller's 'Dolls' Hospital' was a toyshop in Hallgate and once you were inside you walked on, and on, and on past Meccano (advertised by a working model of a giant dockside crane), Hornby trains going round and round, Dinky toys, Tri-Ang pedal cars, prams, wheelbarrows, tricycles, magic lanterns. And you could look longingly at everything even if you couldn't buy until Christmas. Ah, Paradise it was. Sheer bliss. Upstairs, you might just get a glimpse of the older 'Doctor' Meller, sitting in his window, mending dolls, putting on new heads, amputating battered arms and legs and so on, because in those days all dolls seemed to be made of breakable materials.

Scales for weighing loose tobacco, boxes and boxes of cigars, bottles of wine costing a shilling or two... This is the tobacco, wines and spirits counter at Hodgson and Hepworth Ltd, the 'Ready Money Stores' in St Sepulchre Gate. H and H might be likened to today's Sainsburys or Fortnums – a quality store specialising in groceries and 'provisions'. The firm had branches in all the Doncaster suburbs, and some of these buildings – often right off the main thoroughfares – can still be traced though put to other uses.

The firm prided itself on its coffee and tea, but 'Oddy Eppys' sold the most wonderful smoked bacon, too. Their café, with its tiny stage for a three piece orchestra (up the stairs on the right) overlooked the street and was a popular meeting place. Although supermarkets were growing in favour, the clientele liked the personal counter service; they appreciated, too, that the company would deliver ...but by 1979, after changes in ownership and new premises, the last shop had closed and Doncaster had lost a treasured old-fashioned grocer.

Hams, bacon, pork pies... succulent scene at Hodgson and Hepworths in St Sepulchre Gate.

They are the Band of Hope. They have signed The Pledge, and they've borrowed copies of *Hymns Ancient and Modern* off the pews. Now they stand outside Doncaster St George's Parish Church, in good voice, their lamps shining brightly ready to go carol-singing. No date attached but wasn't it that Christmas that ALL the ladies' coat collars were trimmed with fur?

It was 'Doncaster Mutual Co-operative and Industrial Society Limited' in those days, which seems a bit long-winded today. (Imagine writing a cheque!) 'The Stores' or 'Co-op' was how most people abbreviated it. This is the Bentley branch and the advertisements in the windows are for their teas, coffees and cocoas, CWS Pelaw Liquid Metal Polish and Pelaw Cod Liver Oil.

If you wanted it, the Co-op sold it, if not at a branch then in the main shop in town. It was all personal service by the young men in the long white pinafores in the early days, and there was the divi! Can anyone still remember their personal Co-op number, recited every time you made a purchase? (Ours was 20809.)

Doncaster Co-operative Society was founded in the 1860s, its creators being railway employees inspired by the Rochdale pioneers, and thirty years later had a huge new store in the former John Street, used both socially and commercially. At the turn of the century they opened a new building in Station Road, and just after the start of World War Two the present building in St Sepulchre Gate. All the Doncaster Co-op buildings have been impressive, leading the way in distinctive and attractive architecture.

'The Good Sir Jesse Boot' (as D.H.Lawrence called him) opened a shop or two in Frenchgate. You can figure out the date for yourself.

For fresh wet fish you usually went to Doncaster Market Tuesdays and Saturdays, but you could also buy it in many places in town, like Macfisheries in High Street. Also in St Sepulchre Gate where W.D.Borrill (fish and game, tel.401X), and Scarborough Brothers, (fish, fruit, herring curers), are perhaps the best remembered. Was it at Borrill's or Scarborough's where gaping fish lay on the the great wet white marble slabs and there on the wall at the back of the shop was a giant stuffed sturgeon?

Next door to Borrill's in our picture is a shed marked 'Recruiting Office'. Opened presumably for World War One since our picture is undated. Borrills had a second shop in Copley Road.

Doncaster's most famous shop front. (It's only 'arkinson's' on the left window 'cos the 'P' fell off. Must have a word with that over-zealous window cleaner.)

We'll guess this was taken on a Thursday afternoon which was early closing in Doncaster in those far-off days. All the Swiss rolls and sponge cakes have been cleared from the marble window shelves on the right, but tins of humbugs, packets of butter-scotch (dummies, every one!) decorate the left-hand side. Next door is Hepworth's stationers and printers. Hepworths' blinds are down, so it must be Thursday pm. Or maybe it was Sunday. Aren't those lads three choirboys, late for Mattins at St George's?

THE fateful year is 1970 and the corner shop on Morley Road has sold its last packet of Brooke Bond and its last gallon of Pink Paraffin. And there'll be no more dashing along to M.Morris and asking for a tin of Harpic Double Action Cleaner Plus Bleach either – all will be flushed away to widen the road to the extended industrial estate at Wheatley.

Morley Road, from Beckett Road to Wheatley Lane, gets its name from Sir Isaac Morley of Beechfield, Knight, Freeman, Alderman, JP, Mayor of Doncaster 1839 and 1840, director of the Midland Railway, benefactor to 'poor, reduced or decayed persons of Doncaster of good moral character'.

Of course, you knew all that. Just so you don't ever forget the good Sir Isaac we must add it was he who bore a congratulatory address from the inhabitants of Doncaster to the Queen and Prince Albert 'on their providential deliverance from an attempted assassination by a man named Oxford'. The things you can learn from this book!

Entertainment

Pale-faced pierrots and pom-poms – Burton's Bohemians, travelling entertainers, delighted Hexthorpe and Balby with a smile, a song and a dance at Hexthorpe Flatts before World War One. Hexthorpe Flatts were bought by Doncaster Corporation in 1896 as an entertainment centre and holiday attraction easily reached by families of factory workers and railway employees. The quarry on the site became an exquisite sunken garden, famously illuminated each autumn. Boating, bowls, tennis, band concerts, BMX, miniature golf, even a full opera (Wagner's Tannhauser) were among hundreds of entertainments offered over the century.

Roll up, roll up and see Miss Betty Beryl, every boy's sweetheart, star of A.E.Smith's pantomime *Mother Goose* when it visited Doncaster Grand Theatre. What a performance!
'All New Scenery. Splendid New Costumes. Good Specialities. Everything properly managed (No Bungling). Cleanest and Best Organised Pantomime Touring Great Britain today.' Etc, etc. Only the best for the Grand, that's what I say. Good clean fun and No Bungling when our Betty Beryl's about.

'J.Doubtfire and Sons - the Fun Providers' – according to the elaborate lettering across the front. What sort of fun seems in doubt – but coconut shies, most likely. The remaining notices say Ticklers (shades of Ken Dodd), Flowers of all Kinds, and Cigarettes. Almost 100 what look like walking sticks hang from the top rail – can we assume they were prizes for the young sporting gentlemen who showed off their skills at Balby Feast?

John Parr, the former bricklayer turned guitarist and popular singer, stops the traffic in Doncaster High Street. John's 1985 version of the theme to the film *St Elmo's Fire* took him to No.1 in America, and the top ten in Britain. He came to live at Sykehouse, near Doncaster, building his own recording studio and remaining active in the record industry. He wrote the music for the successful film *Three Men and a Baby*.

Shall we dance? What, here in the middle of the street? You press photographers are so persuasive... Graham and June Booth of Park Drive, Sprotbrough, won the UK Senior Intermediate Dance Championship in 1987.

Hot weather, hot music... part of a huge crowd at Doncaster's little Woodstock – the South Yorkshire Jazz Festival in 1975.

Slow, quick quick, slow... and oh so elegant. The singer in her low-cut ball gown, the gentlemen in evening dress... 'LB' on the music stands confirms that this is the Len Boote dance band, billed as King of the Big Band Sound, when they appeared at St James's Baths hall around 1951-52. They played all the halls in and around Doncaster – Mansion House, Baths, Hodgson and Hepworth's in particular. Press balls, works dances, annual hops of this association, that sports club – it always seemed to be Len Boote playing waltz, quickstep, palais glide, veleta, foxtrot. The man himself is the fourth person from the left.

Gordon Bennett! What's this? It's Mr Tuby's Fair at Tickhill. The 'ride' appears to be in racing cars – hence Mr Bennett getting his name in foot-high letters.

The plane trees give it away; they are still there. The cameraman stands on the pavement with Doncaster Conservative Club just showing on the left. The cinema on the right was The Majestic (at the time showing Charles Ruggles in *Charley's Aunt,* billed as 'a laughing mirthquake'). After the Majestic came the Gaumont, re-named the Odeon. Most older people still call this Gaumont Corner.

This gaunt monster, about to be pulled down, is Doncaster's Theatre Royal sandwiched by, on the extreme left A.J.Smith's The Queen public house (aka Arthur Joseph's) and the Woolpack Hotel on the right. Both these establishments are still standing. Today you will market stalls fill much of the space in between. The pic seems to have been taken on a sunny Sunday morr there are so few people about apart from two boys in

entrance roof. The building was opened in 1776, and cost £1,570. By the early 1890s it was described as 'one of the oldest, if not the oldest building of it kind in the country.' All the great Victorian comedians and actors played there. One of the rules of the house was that whistling was forbidden. The Grand Theatre in Station Road replaced it in 1901.

Royal Visits

We know who he is, even after 25 years. But who are they? They'll be 25 years older, too. A youthful and handsome Prince Charles toured the then new Rockware glass factory at Kirk Sandall in 1970. Everyone enjoyed the day, it seems.

Will she, won't she? Every year there was (and still is) speculation about whether the Queen would visit Doncaster for the St Leger. In 1952, the year her father King George VI died, she did join the crowds on Town Moor. But she was an uncrowned monarch when this picture was taken at Bawtry Station saying goodbye to the Earl and Countess Scarbrough.

Royalty did come to Doncaster Races in Edward VII's day. Regularly. The lad leaning on the cart outside the butcher's shop in Doncaster High Street ponders on how the other half lived as his King-Emperor is driven to Doncaster Racecourse. Top left is The Ram Hotel, now The Danum.

Well, don't keep them standing there... are you going to say "Hello Your Majesties" or not? King George V and Queen Mary (we love the hat, Ma'am) wait rigidly for the next move while two of the welcoming party seem at odds about what to do next. The postcard is captioned 'Arrival of Their Majesties at Doncaster' and the date is 1912. King and Queen went on to visit Conisbrough Castle, staying the night at Wentworth Woodhouse. Next day they went to Swinton, Mexborough and the model village at Brodsworth. The visit had its tragic side: they also took the opportunity to visit Cadeby Colliery, where 90 miners had died in two explosions.

When Princess Margaret opened the new Doncaster Museum and Art Gallery in Chequer Road in 1964 (it replaced Beechfield) she also had lunch at Doncaster Mansion House, where another crowd was waiting to see her. Twenty-three years later the Museum was given a purpose-built extension to house the remarkable K.O.Y.L.I. museum, transferred from Pontefract.

King George V and Queen Mary visited Woodlands in the summer of 1912 and toured the new Park 'model village' built for Brodsworth Colliery workers four years earlier. Nobody is waving a flag as the royal limousine purrs through. One or two are raising their hats, one policeman watches with his back to the crowd, who, curious but not obviously enthusiastic, keep a respectful distance. No royal walkabouts in those days!

Another postcard in the 'Conisbrough Royal Visit, 1912' series, this time captioned 'Their Majesties converse with a crippled boy' (perhaps injured in the Cadeby disaster). Crippled is hardly an adjective we would use today.

Transport

Did you have a nice time? What was the weather like? The train from Scarborough and Whitby via York is just in, and they queue for a taxi outside Doncaster Station. Suitcases, holdalls, and a doll's pram are part of the luggage. This was in the days when we could all afford to go by rail – June 1966.

While there are small collections of priceless railway relics in Doncaster, there is no railway museum open to the public – York has all the largest and best LNER and Great Northern material. But for transport enthusiasts in general there remains the Transport Centre at Sandtoft, reached via Hatfield Woodhouse. There are frequent days when trolley buses take passengers on a circular tour, and visitors can look at PSVs of all kinds from many parts of the country, still in their original liveries. Everyone will recognise the red London bus in the centre.

Hodgson and Hepworth were grocers, wine merchants, restaurateurs, bottlers, bacon curers, bakers – they even had a dairy farm. They also provided a horse-drawn bus service. This example is making the return journey probably from Bentley, looking for all the world like the Wild West stage as it passes Killengrey's butterscotch factory in Frenchgate. Trams provided the service a couple of years after this picture was taken.

Tables upside down on top (see all their legs in the air?) Rest of the stuff inside: That's the way to do it. S.Westfield and Sons, furniture removers and steam hauliers 'flit' a family, long ago. 'Move with the Times' is the slogan on the van – and Westfields have kept on doing so. They are still in business in Doncaster.

On 21 February 1916 they opened a tramway route from Doncaster to Woodlands, specially to serve Brodsworth Colliery. The picture shows two conductresses (rare to employ women then?) a conductor, an inspector and a pioneering lady at the helm. The last man to have driven this route told me that you had to stand all the time you drove, that in a thunderstorm, wearing leather, goggles and gauntlets, you still got thoroughly soaked. And nobody wanted to drive the last one to Woodlands on a Saturday night. Some very boisterous people would board the upper deck and soak you unmentionably! Trams could be hazardous in other ways – especially when the tramway was on an incline. The thing gathered momentum and sand boxes which aided braking were not always effective.

A tram! A tram! Flags flutter, small boys look on enviously. Everybody's pushing and shoving to be on Doncaster's first tram, about to move off from the stop outside Doncaster New Grand Theatre in 1902. The Grand Theatre (also called an Electric Picture Palace) is still there... but threatened ('Make a stand for the Grand' is the campaign slogan).

Hang on to your hat, Missus, especially if you going on the top deck. Mind you, the lady looks a little large for climbing anywhere let alone to the the top deck of this open-top tram, even if it is decorated for the Coronation of King George V in 1911. God Save the King and Son Comfort et Liesse*, that's what we say. (* Legend on the former Doncaster County Borough Coat of Arms.)

Ah, messieurs, les aviateurs... the daring young men in the flying machines cement the entente and pose at what was billed as 'The First Aviation Meeting in England – Doncaster race common October 15-23, 1909.' The occasion was a coup for the Corporation – Blackpool wanted to be first! The picture includes the legendary American Col Cody (fourth from left, back row) but the other men were mostly from Europe, especially France. Cody, who the previous year had flown for 27 minutes, was contracted to appear for a fee of £2,000. Many spectators looked upon it as an entertainment, failing to see its frightening scientific and military significance for the future.

The poster that drew 83,000 people to Doncaster Racecourse over eight days. Canvas screens were drawn across the racecourse railings – but this was a flying event. You could see most of what you wanted for nothing!

Roger Sommer's Farman biplane pictured at the Doncaster Aviation meeting of 1909. A draughty machine indeed, it seems little more than sticks, canvas, and engine. The pilot sits forward of the engine (not very safe when you hit something) but this is very much the shape of things to come.

Below: Colonel Cody's machine is towed back to the sheds after giving a display on Doncaster racecourse. The machine appears to be badly damaged. Back to the drawing board, Colonel?

Contact! Chocks away! Monsieur Delagrange's monoplane ready for take off at Doncaster in 1909. A boy in a sailor suit has the honour of holding the tailplane. In the background the racecourse grandstand and the Yorkshire Institution for the Deaf and Dumb, Eastfield House.

These were the trophies for which the daring young men risked their lives in their flying machines at Doncaster Aviation Meeting.

"I name this aircraft Spirit of Doncaster..." The Mayor watched by Alderman Thomson inaugurates a short-lived passenger service from Doncaster Airport.

The good old (but not so old) days at Doncaster. Another transport milestone at the Doncaster works in the 1980s.

Remember the Deltics? That distinctive sound, twin Napier engines giving 3,300 of horse power a-roaring through Doncaster on the East Coast Main Line? With Pinza looking worse for wear in the background, a clutch of cameramen photograph the scene at British Rail Engineering workshops at Hexthorpe when the public was allowed to say farewell to the Deltic locos which had served us so well during the previous 20 years.

Another railway milestone for Doncaster – the last electric locomotive produced at Doncaster leaves the sheds in January 1966.

Two Deltic locomotives were presented to the Deltic Preservation Society in the 1980s. VIPs stand on the rostrum, a man in white coat (looking faintly embarrassed by the business) holds the tape, and *The Alycidon*, growling to be away, nudges through the tape at the British Rail Hexthorpe works.

Stand well back children... the platform's disappeared. But all got on the train – because Askern Station was open for a day in 1974 (it closed in 1947) to allow 200 Askern Spa Club children and parents on their annual outing to Scarborough.

Sorry... after nearly 100 years, there are no more tickets for sale, no more trains stopping here. 'Demolition in progress' reads the sign outside Conisbrough Station in 1986.

A crowd estimated at the time at 50,000 – were there really so many? – watched when Valerie Singleton performed th
ceremony of renaming the LNER locomotive No.532 *Blue Peter*. Miss Singleton was one of the presenters of the childrens
TV programme. The loco was withdrawn from service by 1967 and sold to a *Blue Peter* preservation society which brough
it back to the Plant for overhaul.

The caption reads 'First trip from Tickhill Station, July 6 1910' and half a dozen non-corridor coaches are presumably full of excited 'trippers' (who are probably miners and their families).

Tickhill and Wadworth station, as it was later called, was a 20-minute walk from both Wadworth village and Tickhill township. It was originally part of the South Yorkshire Joint Railway, formed by five companies and coming into operation for freight – principally coal from newly sunk collieries – in 1909. Regular passenger services began in 1910. The first Tickhill stationmaster was one Wilbert Briggs, who was with the company for over 40 years. The SYJR operated between Dinnington and Firbeck Colliery in the southern extreme, and Kirk Sandall in the north. Each company supplied its own locos and rolling stock, the locomotive here being from the Great Central Railway.

The world's most handsome coaches and locomotives were designed and built with meticulous care at Doncaster, and nothing since leads us to change that opinion. Here is *Union of South Africa*, No. 60009, said to be the last steam locomotive to undergo repair at the Plant. The date is 1963. The loco, which went into service in 1937, was withdrawn in 1966 to be preserved privately.

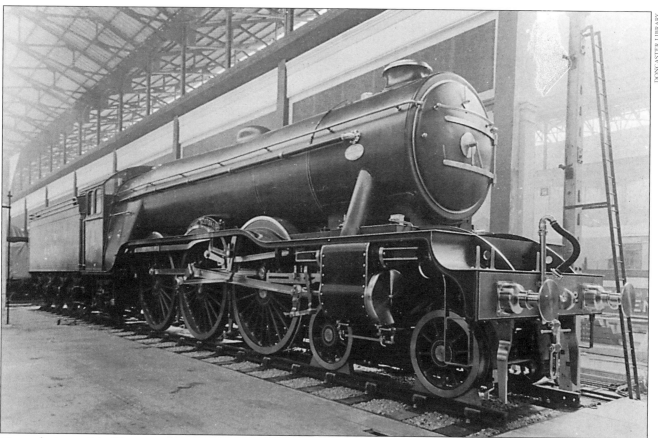

More photographic film must have been exposed on this locomotive than on any other. But why not, isn't it the most famous steam locomotive in the world, and wasn't it built at Doncaster in 1923. There is no date on this photograph of 4472 *Flying Scotsman*, but she (can a Scotsman be a she?) appears to be in pristine condition.

You can see where you are going (Great Central railway map on the wall) and you can see where you've been – because this is a rear observation car, fit for royalty. There's no date on the picture but it is stamped 'L.N.E.R. Drawing Office Photo'. Everything – chairs, lamps, mirror, clerestory, the classical painting, is the work of the artist and master craftsman. Only the nasty common-looking fan adds a jarring note.

Is this King George V's double? Mail vans, with sorting facilities, were first introduced on the railways nearly 150 years ago. Later they had a net collecting apparatus on the side to pick up mail while at speed. Like the water scoop for steam locos, a brilliant idea. But then, all the best ideas are simple ones.

At first glance in looks like the framework for a flimsy garden shed on wheels. At second glance, with that disembodied window-frame thing (centre of picture), it resembles a piece of modern art which everyone understands except me. Both wrong. It's an aeroplane. Isn't that right, Mister Aviator? "Oui, Monsieur" came the deep-throated reply. (Aviators were nearly all foreigners in those days.) Occasion was the famous Doncaster flying meeting of 1909.

Without doubt, this was shape of things to come. Another contestant at the Doncaster competitive flying meeting of 1909. Many shapes and sizes appeared at that famous meeting but this state-of-the-art design (propeller up front, then engine, then pilot behind) was the one which many aircraft manufacturers would follow in years to come.

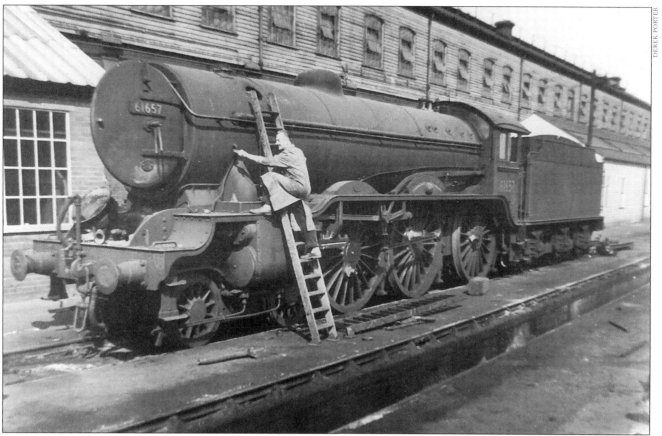

It's sort of 'half-time' for *Doncaster Rovers*, having been run ragged on the railway for a long long time. 'Rovers' (No. 61657 as every spotter who ever stood on Hexthorpe Bridge could have told you) was back in the dressing-room at the Doncaster works for repair when this picture was taken. You may just recognise the brass half-a-football over the second driving wheel which gave this class of loco such distinction.

Are they lined up for scrap, or are they waiting to have their thingummies replaced, and the bits and bobs screwed back on? A dozen identical locomotives, led by Henry A.Ivatt's 4-2-2 No.264, have finished their useful life and come home to die. Ivatt's engine looks very similar to one of his predecessor Patrick Stirling's 8ft 'Singles'. The locomotives in our picture, taken in 1918, await the dismantler's torch after only 17 years' service.

Horse Racing

Notebooks and pencils ready, lads. Here they come! Perhaps there was no photo-finish equipment when Ballymoss (T.Burns) won the 1957 St Leger at Doncaster from Court Harwell (A.Breasley) and Brioche (E.Hide).

The winning post writes the caption for us – the 205th St Leger, 1981. A lone policeman surveys a tightly-packed crowd making their last-minute bets.

Doncaster won the Racecourse of the Year award in 1975 and there was no better person to receive it than Councillor Albert Cammidge, chairman, centre right, who had become renowned throughout the industry. Extreme right is Don Cox, the racecourse manager. The award was made by the Racegoers Club.

Smart press photographer finds a new angle! At an exhibition of racing pictures and memorabilia, a portrait of Elis, a St Leger winner, is photographed through the spokes of a wheel taken from the first recorded horsebox!

Well done! Mrs Charles Englehard pats Indiana after the horse won the St Leger of 1964.

Easy! Nothing to it! Never Say Die wins the St Leger by a mile and the jockey has time to smile for the cameramen.

Cantelo joins the Hall of St Leger fame. The horse is led into the winner's enclosure in 1959. Eddie Hide is the jockey.

THIS INN
IS THE BIRTHPLACE
OF
THE ST. LEGER

THE RACE WAS PROPOSED
BY LT.~GEN. A. ST. LEGER
AT A SUPPER PARTY HERE
IN 1776, WAS FIRST RUN
IN THAT YEAR, AND WAS
GIVEN IT'S NAME AT A
DINNER PARTY AT
THIS INN IN 1778

TO MARK THE
BICENTENARY OF THE
NAMING OF THE RACE
THIS PLAQUE WAS PLACED
HERE ON
21ST SEPTEMBER 1978

This plaque, which speaks for itself, was unveiled by Moya Frenze St Leger in the Red Lion Hotel in Doncaster Market Place. There is, however, controversy over details. Others will claim that it was at a dinner at Warmsworth Hall in 1776 when Lord Rockingham asked a group of influential gentlemen to collect a sweepstake amongst themselves and institute a race to be called after the name of their host, Colonel St Leger, who was living at Warmsworth at the time.

The St Leger Day scene on Town Moor in 1959. All the men appear to be wearing trilbies and smart suits. The few women punters all wear hats.

'The crowd on the common, Coronation Day'. The common is the centre of the racecourse, the coronation that of George V, the date 1911. Not a bare head anywhere.

'There's all sorts o' committees you can be on, sithee lad. Sanitary, Waterworks, Gas, Watch... but we're t'Race Committee and that's best on all on 'em, 'cos you get Free Race Tickets! And no, we're not bunching up for thee to take us picture, young man. Tha'll tek us as we are. We're t'Race Committee.

'Proud? O'course we're proud. Racecourse is OUR racecourse. Belongs to Doncaster, see. Quarter of a million watch Leger. Hundreds of train-loads, from all ower t'country. Thousands and thousands of 'em come for t' Gold Cup an' all. That's munny for Donny, that is, lad, and don't thee forget it. Just you see what'll 'appen in next 20 years ...new grandstands, new enclosure, new saddling paddock, straight mile. We're t' Race Committee, keeping t' rates down.'
– The date is 1895. The population of the borough was about 26,000.

DONCASTER LIBRARY

Focus your binoculars, everyone, and eyes left. Here they come! It's King Edward VII and friends at Doncaster Races (HM on the right, centre). This was his last visit to Town Moor. He died that year, 1910.

DONCASTER LIBRARY

Noble Lord, accosting attractive young Honourable in the Paddock after the first race: "Greetings dear lady. Your smile tells me you backed the winner? One o' mine, ye know. Bought her at Tattersalls couple of years ago. They tell me I've an eye for a good filly!"

Young Hon., meanwhile, knows all about aforesaid Noble Lord and young fillies, and smiles her reply.

Noble Lord: "Didn't I see you with young what's-is-name at the Leger Dinner last night? Aren't you and Reggie supposed to be enga…" Our Young Hon.'s reply will never be known because at that moment up pops our happy snapper who has been promised two guineas by the Picture Editor of the *Sketch* for a good 'un, and this looks like it. Lord Lonsdale is the Noble Lord. The identity of the young lady is not known to us.

This is Tattersalls bloodstock sales, and in the background we can still recognise it as 'Harwood's Terrace' or the northern side of Waterdale. The auctioneer would be in the rather shabby wooden building, on the left. The area of Waterdale, or Horse Fair, was traditionally the scene for much buying and selling of horses. It was also said in years gone by to be a venue for cock fighting, rowdy political rallies, rioting and all manner of public displays and excesses. Later it was smart residential; still later a bus station. Now a car park.

Just a section of the huge crowd which watched the St Leger a hundred years ago. There is feverish activity in front of the bookmakers who line the iron railing, everyone looking at his racecard or counting his money. This was the crowd, probably twice what we see at a Cup Final today, which made the 'Yorkshire Roar' so famous. Meanwhile, five bobbies of the Borough Force walk the course – we would like to think, to the cheers of the crowd.

Bit late now to put on a bet. You'd never get through the crush to the bookmakers, who are just dimly visible in the misty top right of this St Leger meeting picture dated 1936. The crowd – nearly all are men – is on what was then the free course. When we were young we would be here as soon as they had dispersed – looking for pennies, threepenny bits, tanners and bobs trampled in the grass. For the sharp-eyed, it could be very profitable.

The Vasey family of Doncaster figured prominently in the history of the turf and here Mr Vasey supervises an early-morning training exercise on the misty Town Moor. Note the V on the saddle cloth.

Street Scenes

Farewell Fitzwilliam Street! What Hitler couldn't do, the demolishers did. Dad takes a last lingering look. Maybe he was born in that bedroom now open to the skies.

Cottages in Bennetthorpe near the Rockingham Hotel. There is no date on the photograph, but the H-shaped TV aerial gives a clue.

Elegance and symmetry in stone. Pity about the ugly plumbing. This is Regent Square, thankfully little changed.

North Bridge, which takes a main road over the South Yorkshire Navigation and the East Coast Main Railway, has been extensively rebuilt in recent times, and today, while retaining those distinctive umbrella-like arches, has attractive brickwork and lighting – a great – improvement on a rather grim structure.

This is how the bridge looked in 1974, over 65 years after it had been built. (Note those distinctive spikey railings which deterred the most adventurous.) The steps just visible in the foreground led to the towpath and to what was once the northern bus station. In the background is the then-controversial North Bridge car park. A level crossing originally carried the old Great North Road across the Great Northern line at this point, causing aggravating delay to increasing north-south road traffic. Essential as the bridge now seems, Doncaster Corporation was not very keen on having a 'New Bridge' and a poll was taken among the ratepayers. There were 1,683 were in favour, 1,513 against.

Another view of North Bridge, looking north, captioned by the photographer 'The New Bridge, Doncaster' with 'the old way' on the right. A tram heads down the middle of the road towards Woodlands. Building on the skyline, centre right, is the former Brown Cow public house.

The entrance to Doncaster Racecourse – viewed across the former Horse Shoe Pond. This area is today's traffic roundabout with Bennetthorpe on the left, Bawtry Road on the right and and Carr House Road behind us. Legend has it that welshing bookmakers were chased this way by furious punters and, if caught, thrown into the pond.

Jubilee Road, Wheatley, in pristine condition, with all the garden walls and iron railings intact. And in the days when you could leave your bike, horse, dray, and handcart unattended without fear of it vanishing. Across the side street that's Stuart's, where they sold hats, coats, shirts and unmentionables. This side the sign advertises 'table waters' – posh name for pop, fizz, minerals.

Demolition work in progress on the Doncaster ring road. The Parish Church helps us to recognise the scene with, just to the right of it, St George's School. Centre right is the Public Library (built 1889) in St George Gate, about to b[e] destroyed. Left is the garage of E.W.Jackson in wha[t] remains of lower French Gate. Mr Jackson set up h[is]

Cheswold works here in 1904 and by the start of World War One had produced almost 100 cars, the last of which – a magnificent example of an early motor car – can be seen today in Doncaster Museum, Chequer Road. Middle left is part of Mr Hanley's flour mill built in the 1920s which, like almost everything else on this picture is no longer there.

Down the Pit

Thirsty work, mining! Men prepare to go underground at a colliery near Doncaster.

Edlington Colliery as it looked in the 1920s. Now but a memory.

Show your faces only, lads, and smile nicely for the cameraman. Some of us are so modest! The picture was taken at a pithead baths 'somewhere in Doncaster'.

Brodsworth colliery yard in 1952. Deserted. Not a miner in sight, not a picket, not even a single seller of a *Socialist Worker*. They're all strangely absent, in a dispute involving a Jugoslav worker the details of which are buried deep in the archives. But who's that in the Al Capone-era motor car? They used to call Broddie The Queen's Pit because they said that's where her coal came from. So maybe it's the Queen's coalman, wondering when he's going to get the next sackful. Closer examination under the magnifier suggests it's a taxi. Brodsworth Colliery closed in September 1990, 85 years after Charles Thellusson, of Brodsworth Hall, had cut the first turf. The first coal was brought up in 1907.

It says on the back of this one 'King George VI and Queen Elizabeth at Hickleton Colliery'. No date, but the occasion could be one of those tours of the country made by Their Majesties to boost morale in the darker days of World War Two.

They called them Merry-go-Round trains in 1966 when this picture was taken – keeping a constant flow of coal from the pits to the power stations. Dl895 is pictured returning for more coal from Highgate Colliery. That was in the merry old days when everyone wanted more and more coal.

Everyone loves a set of 'going, going... now you see it, now you don't' photographs. This little sequence shows the blasting of a concrete settling tank at Markham Main Colliery, Armthorpe, in 1977. The funnel-shaped tank defied four attempts to blow it up (or is it blow it down?) and the picture below shows the fifth and successful explosion.

Another in the 'going, going' series; this time Cadeby Colliery chimney bites the dust. Fred Dibnah, where were you?

Cadeby Colliery – chimney intact – in 1983.

Like a still from an epic film they march to the pit head to wait, and to hope. But there would be very little news to cheer them. This is the scene on the road to Cadeby pit after South Yorkshire's worst colliery disaster when 88 men and boys died.

Bentley with Arksey Heritage Society was formed in 1988, and members have mounted frequent public displays. In our 1990 picture, Deborah Hagland and Patrick Madden are seen with some of the Bentley disaster memorial items.

Happy days, unhappy days at Bentley Colliery. Bentley miners celebrated a 25,975 tonnes production record in 1989. Perhaps the feat is forgotten now. Yet no one ever forgets the two major disasters at the pit; in 1931 when 45 miners died after an explosion, and 1978, when seven were killed. A memorial in Arksey cemetery is dedicated to all of them, and our second picture shows the laying of wreaths in 1981, 50 years after the first tragedy.

Either it's Sunday morning and they're all at church and why not. Or there's free beer at the Big Drum. Or there's Phyllis Dixie dancing the Seven Veils at the Grand. Or everyone's hard at work below ground at Bentley Colliery. Wherever they are, that chimney's belching full blast.

Walter Sanderson and Darkie, a pit pony from Bentley, appeared at Wickersley Show in 1965.

Rossington miners' children queue for bread during the General Strike of 1926. The strike followed an ultimatum to the nation's miners that unless they accepted wage cuts and longer hours, then they would be deemed to be locked out of work.

So the strike began at midnight on 3 May, 40,000 Doncaster trade unionists came out in sympathy, and there were violent confrontations in South Yorkshire. After nine days the TUC called the strike off – leaving the miners to carry on alone until forced back to work by privation.

The picture that writes its own caption. Rossington Colliery had been productive for 72 years when this record tonnage was reached.

"Now where do you want it? Here?" "No, bit to your right, Joe." Joe (feeling the pressure of the occasion) "Here then?" "Aye, reckon tha's about reight, start there."

It's a chilly morning at Stainforth and they are about to dig the first turf for Hatfield Colliery and so change the face of the countryside seemingly for ever.

With solemn tread and slow... corteges are taken through the streets of Denaby. There appear to be six glass-sided hearses on this photogaph captioned 'Funeral Denaby Victims' – presumably of a colliery accident.

Denaby Main produced 50 million tons of coal before it closed in 1968. More than 200 miners had lost their lives there and about the same number were killed at the associated Cadeby Main. When two explosions shook Cadeby in 1912, 88 men and boys were killed, so the scenes like this must have been all too common.

Don't they look just lovely! Throw a little more water on the hot stones, brother. Miners at Hatfield enjoy that old Finnish custom, a sauna bath. And followed, we trust, by the cold plunge. Here then are the newly-washed; our other picture shows six of the unwashed, descending 'the steps in an orderly manner for safety's sake' (just as the notice says they should), and making for that invigorating delight, the sauna. The date is May 1971.

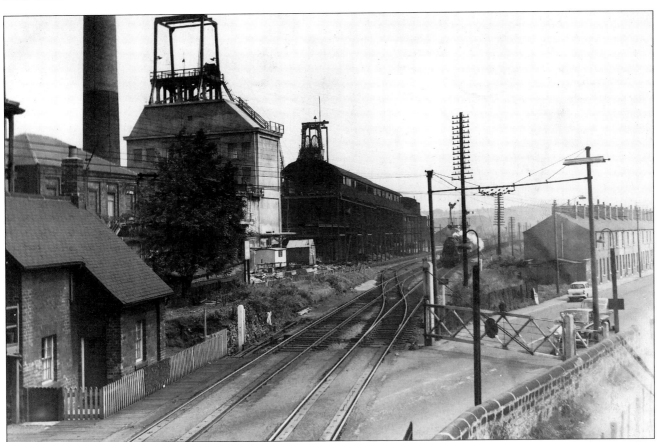

There have been so many strikes. long or lightning, at South Yorkshire collieries in the last hundred years that nobody can possibly remember them all. This picture of Denaby Main by the level crossing was taken in August 1960. The photographer's caption reads 'Strike over one man... the quiet of Denaby Main this afternoon.' Not so very quiet; there's a freight train a-coming.

Surely a sentence, if not a chapter of coal-mining history, here. This is a 150hp trepanshearer in use on 6's and 7's unit in the High Moor seam at Denaby Main Colliery in 1965. The roof is supported by Dobson five-leg powered supports and the coal leaves the face on a 30-inches wide armoured face conveyor. This face, as the man at the colliery explained to us, was one of the longest in the country at 365 yards, and was the first in Yorkshire to have Dobson five-leg supports fitted. And that, even to we ignorant surface workers, is perfectly understandable. Good for you, Dobson. Sorry we don't know the name of the operator.

No wonder he's smiling; another strike at Askern is over and he's back at work. The year is 1974.

Maureen Bell of Cudworth was Yorkshire Miners' Coal Queen in 1983. Here she waits for her train at Doncaster *en route* to the national finals in Blackpool. Pushing a porter's barrow and helping her with her luggage are Mr Simon Ward, then area terminal manager of British Rail, and Mr Ray Hemsley, station supervisor at Doncaster.

Askern Colliery after the strike of 1974. Easy to tell they are heading for the coal face.

Fifteen regional Coal Queens held court for a photo call at Coal House, Doncaster, in September 1971 before going to Skegness for the national final. Yorkshire Coal Queen that year was Julia Baker (front of picture), aged 20, of Bolton-on-Dearne.

Jackie Barnard was Cadeby Colliery Coal Queen in 1982.

Smile, lads, Joe's got a bottle of something stronger than cold tea and so has Harry and it's a lovely sunny day to take a drop as well as to take a walk. We don't know the circumstances but these Bentley Colliery surface workers look happy in anticipation. The year is 1920.

The people watch in silence. Only the sound of the lorries' engines, only the rhythmic marching of the St John Ambulancemen, solemn and slow, as the victims of the Bentley Colliery explosion of 1931 are taken to Arksey cemetery.

The Miners' Strike of 1984

The year-long national miners' strike in 1984 against contraction of the coal industry was perhaps the most momentous struggle in trade union history. Much of it centred around Doncaster, at the heart of the industry, and its impact on families, between neighbours, on trade, and on all walks of pit village life was immeasurable. Hundreds of policemen from distant forces were embroiled, and memories of the violent struggle remain as everlasting 'images of Doncaster'.

The bitterness that had lingered after the 1926 débàcle was revived after the defeat of 1984 and subsequent events have shown that most of the predictions about the fate of the industry were in fact unhappily true. These scenes at the pit gate are typical of the time; the roughly-built shelter, the brazier, the police often helmeted and holding riot shields, opposing angry young men. This was the picture at Rossington in July, when two officers faced the anger of the crowd. In our other picture, the glare of the street lamps dramatises events at Denaby.

Pickets and supporters erected barricades at Rossington.

NUM officials were tireless in organising the strike and alleviating hardship. Here Dearne Valley NUM branch secretary Eric Mountain, wrapped against the cold of January, finds a little warmth by the pickets' brazier.

Mr Dennis Skinner, MP for Bolsover, walks alongside Trade Union leader Rodney Bickerstaffe in front of a vivid Sheffield Women Against Pit Closure banner during the 1993 protest.

Some didn't want to strike, tried to work, braved the inevitable taunts and insults... and accepted the consequences in a community that did not forget easily.

There had been soup kitchens in Bentley 60 years before... that postcard scene showing loaves of bread being handed out to the children was not forgotten. But now, to everyone's horror, history was repeating itself. Striking miners in 1984 are served bread, beans, sausage and scrambled egg by women who wear metal badges which urge 'Coal Not Dole' and 'Support the Miners against Pit Closures'.

The strike was over, but the struggle continued. And, as ever, the women fought as strongly as their menfolk. Here Women Against Pit Closures campaigner Brenda Nixon of Thorne is pictured with Dennis Skinner at a rally in Doncaster in 1993.

The Rossington marchers. The face of white-haired veteran Jock Kane, one-time popular Communist and prominent Armthorpe NUM branch official, is centrepiece of the Armthorpe branch banner.

They marched down High Street attracting the sympathy of the onlookers. Doncaster MP Sir Harold Walker (bareheaded) is in the midst of them.

This was the scene outside Markham Main, Armthorpe, when the pit was closed amid stormy scenes in 1992. 'The World for the Workers' is the optimistic proclamation by the Hatfield Main contingent.

But all was not to remain doom and gloom. By June 1995 Markham Main general manager Jonathan Oxby was able to announce the creation of 50 new jobs at the former British Coal colliery.

Industry

The scene is Parkinson's sweet factory, 1969. The girls appear to be making something like peppermint creams – but whatever they are doing it looks a pretty boring job. Sam Parkinson began making sweets in Doncaster in 1817 at the back of his shop in High Street, in particular his famous Doncaster butterscotch, or 'Royal Doncaster Butterscotch' as it became once Queen Victoria had presumably peeled away the silver paper and sucked a slab in 1851.

Despite intense competition from other Doncaster sweet makers – Killingrey, Nuttal, and 'Toffee' Jackson among many – Parkinsons expanded worldwide.

Their humbugs, fruit drops, and baking powder were all famous. But none so famous as the scotched or scorched crunchy butterscotch, endorsed by royalty, nobility, clergy and gentry. The butterscotch, once in its familiar white

paper wrapper, was a particular favourite among the crowds in Leger Week. The factory meanwhile had moved to Wheatley and the High Street premises became a shop selling bread and cakes, and restaurant. This building, although since 1960 no longer Parkinsons, escaped demolition thanks to Doncaster Civic Trust and it continues to look attractive.

The blackboard declares them to be 'Woodhouse, Osborne, & Coy, Brass Finishers, Hexthorpe'. Is that Mr Woodhouse on the left, Mr Osborne on the right, and the entire Coy?

You can almost hear the rumble of great wheels a-turning. This is Wiltons mustard mill, on the banks of the River Don, perhaps once a rival to Mr Colman? The two men hold soft hand-brushes presumably to sweep clear the milled mustard.

Churches

John Jarratt made his fortune as a partner in the manufacturer of iron, and gave £13,000 for the building of Christ Church, Doncaster. The foundation stone was laid in 1827, the first service was held there in 1829 but Jarratt did not live to see the completion of the work, having died at his house in St Sepulchre Gate in 1828, aged 84.

Earlier, Jarratt had established his Charity Fund of 1821, which paid out every month to 'six poor, reduced or decayed persons aged 50-plus of good moral character and residing within the town of Doncaster as shall be thought the most proper and deserving.'

Christ Church, a much-enjoyed building, but now abandoned by the Anglicans, continues to adorn that western end of Thorne Road. Jarratt, meanwhile, gives his name to a street in Hyde Park.

MR MALCOLM JOHNSTON

And any moment now a Great Big Hairy Spider will come out and get you! The view is through the windows of the Frenchgate Centre with St George's Church in the background.

When a fault in a heating system set fire to front pews on the south side of the nave at Doncaster Parish Church the damage might at first have seemed comparatively minor. After all, the whole church was destroyed by fire in 1853. The charred woodwork in this picture was effectively repaired, but the smoke given off proved the real problem, and the huge Edmund Schulze organ, one of the wonders of Doncaster, although many yards from the fire, required extensive and expensive cleaning. The Vicar, the Rev John Bird, is seen examining the pew which is reserved for the Mayor of Doncaster. The ironwork is designed to hold the civic mace.

It says 'The New Church Edlington'. The photographer wrote his own caption. Pity he didn't also give us the date.

Going to War

Don't shoot until you see the whites of their eyes, men, and have the cold steel ready! The West Yorkshire Home Guard prepare to repel an imaginary foe advancing on dear old Donny. The date must be 1940-something.

A huge crowd, some of them clinging to the railway station roof, greeted the return of South Yorkshire's Boer War veterans. The war began in 1899 and by the peace of Vereeniging in 1902 British casualties were 7,000 killed with 13,000 dead of disease. The Boers lost 26,000 – 20,000 of disease in British concentration camps. So there is a sombre appearance to our procession. As the town's constables lead the way a solitary flag flies over the station. No bunting, no band, just a sense of thankfulness that it's all over, rather than triumphant jubilation.

Ooh, look Mother, there's our Alfie. 'im with the 'at on... This is the Doncaster Battalion Royal Engineers (not forgetting the dog, front centre). They are seen with the Mayor at Doncaster Racecourse before going to France in 1914. Sadly, we have to wonder how many of them came back...

'E.L.S.' captioned this 'Doncaster Territorials at Sprotbrough Church, November 15, 1908.' Can't see the church and can't recognise the lane down which they follow the band. Can you?

Carol Hill, Doncaster's local history librarian, and Keeper
of many of the photographs in this book, dates this picture
as early 1890s – because the clock (centre, far distan e) has
not been replaced by the one of 1895 – the one which we
know best on the site today. The soldiers are the Yorksh
Dragoons, who had their headquarters in the town. Tall
building on the left is the Mansion House, the dark sto
pillared building to the left of it the Subscription Room

On the right is the Doncaster Lyceum, originally the home of a local scientific society, later (like the Subscription Rooms) a betting room and – within the memory of many of us – the former Lyceum Restaurant. Small boys congregate by the pump outside The Ram (today's Danum Hotel). A dragoon was a mounted infantryman carrying a ligh automatic rifle.

"Right then, sergeant, get the men to fall in." (Captain Mainwaring, where are you now?)

This may have been one of the last parades of a section of the Doncaster Plant Works Home Guard, numbering in total over 500 men, when the picture was taken in 1944. By that time the war on the European mainland was going well. 'Mister Hitler' was retreating in Normandy, Rome had surrendered and there had been landings in Southern France. Amazingly, the Plant escaped damage by enemy aircraft – their bombs didn't explode – but accidental fire destroyed the carriage shop soon after World War Two was declared.

The writing on the back leads us to believe it is a National Savings campaign sometime in 1944-45. On the steps of the Corn Exchange (Exchange Restaurant entrance) stands Alderman Trotter, the Mayor, urging us to buy Savings Certificates. The legend adds: 'Ethel Buck in turret of second tank (Matilda.)' Now Ethel was at that time the famous 'Mother Hubbard' who wrote a children's column for the *Doncaster Gazette*. She was a prolific journalist, specialising in amateur theatre and children's subjects, and in her later years became librarian of the *Doncaster Evening Post* on North Bridge.

Civic Affairs

You voted them in... and maybe you voted some of them out! This is Doncaster Metropolitan District Council photographed in Doncaster Mansion House in 1974.

The Mayor and Corporation of Doncaster, as seen in 1909. The picture was taken in the Guildhall Yard.

Telling the News

For many years Doncaster had two evening newspapers – the *Yorkshire Evening Post* printed in Scot Lane together with its associated weekly the *Doncaster Chronicle*, and the *Yorkshire Evening News* in Printing Office, where the *Doncaster Gazette* was published.

First to fold was the Conservative *Chronicle*, followed by the Leeds-based *News*, followed by the *Gazette*. The *Yorkshire Evening Post* (S Yorks Edition) meanwhile became the *Doncaster Evening Post*, printed and published on North Bridge, and it, too, is no more. These pictures show all these newspaper offices and the final demolition scene on North Bridge.

The *Doncaster Evening Post* editorial and printing works was a former road transport depot, and the garage for the company's delivery vans on a site nearer St Mary's Bridge had been a huge stables before the car began to dominate road transport. There were still wide inclined roadways to the upper storey, where once the horses had been taken. The heads of horses carved on a gable end are just visible.

When it was clear that the *Doncaster Evening Post* would be forced to close down, strenuous effort was made by *The Star* to ensure that Doncaster would continue to have an evening newspaper without any interruption in the service. Some members of staff moved from North Bridge to Sheffield where the new newspaper would be produced; others stayed on in Doncaster, to be accommodated in temporary buildings in – of all places – the grounds of Doncaster Rovers FC at Belle Vue. And so *The Doncaster Star* was born. Meanwhile a 'proper office' was being made ready in the former Cuttriss Brothers toys and model shop in Duke Street, and our picture shows the opening ceremony in January 1984.

Doncaster continues to enjoy its own evening newspaper without interruption; a tradition which began in the 1920s moves towards the next millenium, thanks to *The Star.*

Healing the Sick

This was Doncaster General Infirmary and Dispensary in Whitaker Street, built in 1868 for £5,466. It replaced the old Dispensary, a medical charity in French Gate, and was itself replaced by the present Royal Infirmary on Thorne Road. It has been used for many things – a school, billets for soldiers, the education offices – and was suddenly and surprisingly pulled down in recent times. The sketch was made soon after the infirmary was opened when there were 25 beds for in-patients, a house surgeon's residence, a physician's room, a surgeon's room, dispensary and kitchens.

Doncaster Healthcare NHS Trust administrative headquarters are in St Catherine's House, Tickhill Road, Balby, in the centre of a huge and nationally famous hospital complex. The building with its blanked side windows, and half a dozen crenellated ornamental towers is posh fancy ashlar stone at the front, and cheaper plain brick at the rear, as this one reveals. If the stone had not turned so black and so patchy, it might be more attractive. But we don't suppose the Trust has time to worry about that sort of triviality.

Doncaster from the Air

Aerial views give us an entirely new perspective, and show just how much room is taken up by modern roads and car parks. Here is St George's Church, with part of Hanley's mill by the canal still standing, and North Bridge car-park bottom right. The white patch was the site of Greyfriars Baths. Much of this area has been redeveloped. In the far distance, Doncaster Royal Infirmary.

133

The same area today, looking north. Again, we can take our bearings from St George's Church. The Corn Exchange (centre left) has a temporary covering after the fire of 1994.

Waterdale showing Coal House from a different angle on the left, police HQ and Doncaster College lower right, Co-op building top centre.

The East Coast
Main Line, crossed
by North Bridge.
The South
Yorkshire
Navigation cuts
underneath both
road and railway.
The old *Doncaster
Evening Post*
building, formerly
a British Road
Transport depot, is
top left. The
picture was taken
in 1979.

Sprotborough 1980 looking East with Crimpsall Ings power station (now demolished) top right.

Another 1980 picture taken from the Goodyear Airship Europa (a part of which you can see top right) shows Balby Bridge, with the Old Cemetery right. The East Coast Main Line runs diagonally.

Woodlands 1980 with the colliery that gave it life – Brodsworth Main – top centre.

Bessacarr with Cantley Bridge centre, left, and the end of The Oval just visible lower left.

Wadworth

Wadworth Hall, believed to have been designed by James Paine. Paine, of Wragby, was largely responsible for Doncaster Mansion House (completed around 1749), Nostell Priory, Cusworth Hall, Serlby Hall, Worksop Manor and Sandbeck. Our picture is dated 1969.

A *Doncaster Star* photographer took this one in Wadworth in 1990, when Wadworth Parish Council were determined that the traditional red telephone box should not be replaced by any nasty modern thing. There it stands outside the White Hart; fitting happily into the landscape. Down with 'progress' we say.

May Day celebrations in Wadworth moved away from the busy main street in later years and this was the scene on the safer playing field of Wadworth First and Middle School in 1988. The pole was not so high, but the decoration remains similar. A bouncy castle in the background adds to a sense of fun and freedom.

Thorne

Ascend the tower of the Parish Church of St Nicholas, Thorne, and (they say) you can see six rivers (that's what they say anyway). And what would the rivers be called? Why, the Humber, Don, Went, Ouse, Trent and Aire. Perhaps it has to be a VERY clear day.

Certainly, if you look immediately south from the tower you can see a grassy earthwork called Peel Hill, site of a moated castle in the twelfth century. It never figured much in history, but it was where they kept the poachers when poaching was a very serious crime indeed. Not much left to see today – except the hill. Our picture was taken in 1983. Still a few poachers about.

Thorne was always famous for its boats and boatyards, like Stanilands and Dunstans. You could go to London, and Europe, indeed anywhere by water from Thorne at one time. They got a canal in the late eighteenth century; steam packets plied from Waterside; they built keels, paddle steamers and even a man o' war in Nelson's time. And in the last war Dunstans were launching a new vessel, which had arrived in sections, every six days. Pleasure craft were beginning to dominate when this picture of Stanilands boatyard was taken in 1965.

And if you are very good, you can feed the ducks! And I might buy you an iced lolly. Mum takes a walk in Thorne Memorial Park in 1971. Let's hope there were some ducks.

They have built ships – sometimes big ships – in Thorne for a very long time. Humber Keels were to the design of the Vikings. And tugs, trawlers, working boats, Admiralty orders destined for faraway places... all were made at Thorne, one time or another. Launched 'em sideways, see. A big splash and you got wet if you were watching and weren't careful. Here H302 *Burton Pidsea* looks ready for the next stage of construction. Burton Whatsea? It's a farming village east of Hull. The picture was taken in 1976.

It's Thorne Market Place. And not so long ago, either; 1960s, we think. 'Rayners cycle works' it says on the roof in the background. That's not there any more but the stalls look much the same today, and it's still an awkward rapid right, left, for through traffic, just as it probably was 400 years ago when the first market was held on this spot. Darley's, the former Thorne brewers, supplied the ales to the White Hart.

When they 'ran them in' in Thorne, this is where then ran them in to. It's Thorne's old police station and lock-up on Silver Street. It was built in 1866 and seen here for sale in 1991.

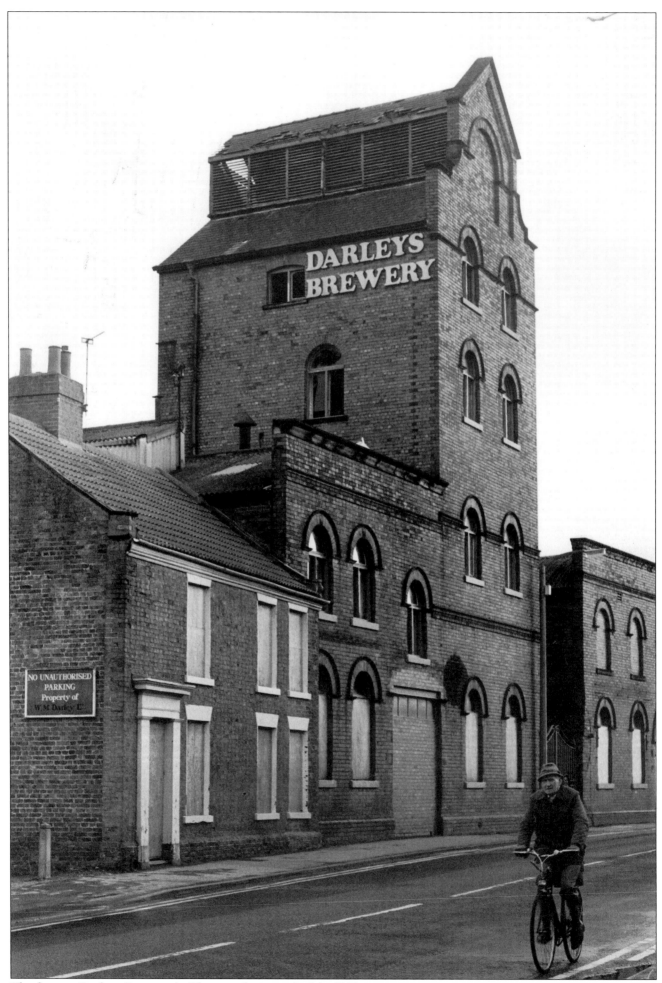

The former Darleys Brewery in Thorne, photographed in 1991.

Up anchor, let go your whatsit, haul in the thingie. Young Sea Cadets wait for a breeze during a Staniland Yacht Club and Doncaster Sailing Club rally at Thorne in 1967. Think on: That's nearly 30 years ago. They could be vice-admirals now.

Tickhill

Tickhill Buttercross was erected in 1777 and restored nearly 100 years ago. Street furniture rather spoils the symmetry of a delightful centre-piece.

Tickhill Castle is open to the public one day a year, and our view is from the motte looking down to the most dramatic, though hidden, structure still standing which is the gatehouse on the left. The castle, rather more than Conisbrough, has a 'wartime' history. It was captured by King John and besieged in the Civil War. Hence that 'knocked abaht a bit' appearance. The house within the walls is inhabited, and is a much later addition.

Tickhill mill dam, reached either behind the Millstone Hotel, or via Dam Road, is a popular venue of artists and photographers. Sit on any seat here, open a paper bag – and just wait for the rush of hungry ducks!

Sprotborough

Sprotbrough lock in 1978. Sprotbrough now has a computerised lock, one of many such high-tech innovations and built as part of a £15m scheme to improve the South Yorkshire Navigation canal.

'Do not pick flowers, start fires, or leave litter!' Let's hope somebody took some notice. Sprotbrough Flash Nature Reserve on washland by the River Don was officially opened by Councillor Willers in June 1984.

Ferry Boat Cottage, Sprotbrough, photographed in 1987.

Street scene, Sprotbrough, one June day in 1972. Such places change very little.

This one was sent to us by the Doncaster Community Programme Agency in 1988, so we'll use their caption which reads: 'During a five-week period, a four-man team from the Agency moved the 100-year-old Sprotbrough pump. A joint venture financed by local businessman Mr Trevor Miller, pictured with Agency Supervisor John Sigsworth, moved the pump and stone surround the half mile to its new home in front of the old rectory.' A nice piece of work, and the two men seem to be pumping hard... but we can't see any water. The arms are of the Copley family, whose family seat was the former Sprotbrough Hall, now demolished.

The road bridge over the South Yorkshire Navigation at Sprotbrough, with the *Enterprise* pushing up stream towards Mexborough. The year is 1990.

Everyone who had a camera, everyone who painted, who sought a little tranquility or a place for a spot of courting made his way down those hairpin bends deep into the Don Gorge, and Sprotbrough was the most delectable and romantic of venues. Later quarrying spoiled the scene, but the charm of the place remains to this day. Here a Humber Keel lowers sail and drops the mast to pass beneath the bridge on which our cameraman stands.

Conisbrough

Conisbrough castle, following very extensive restoration, is now being promoted as never before. Just how magnificent the place is, and well worth a visit, is well illustrated by this aerial picture with church, castle and tent-like visitor centre prominent. The flats, however, so very twentieth century, are in marked contrast to the 90ft high, twelfth-century keep built by Henry II's half brother Hameline Plantagenet.

Stick one on 'im. Go on... dare you. Making no attempt at peacemaking between Dave Haywood and John Pilkington are English Heritage chairman Jocelyn Stevens, Ivanhoe Trust director Stuart Davy, trust chairman Dr David Davis and Doncaster council leader, Councillor Peter Welsh. The combatants are tour guides. The occasion was the official re-opening of the Castle in April 1995 after a £350,000 facelift.

Three views for the price of one, here. Conisbrough Castle with the King George V Coronation Fountain of 1911, and the World War One-style soldier War Memorial. The picture was taken in 1971.

Edgar Scrivens, recorder of South Yorkshire's last days of rural innocence, took this well-known photograph of the uphill road out of Conisbrough looking east towards Doncaster. Extreme left is a cycle dealer and hirer; halfway up the hill is the Star Inn.

Sporting Days

Boxing:

Bruce Woodcock became Doncaster's favourite son in the heady post-war period when all of us badly needed heroes and something or somebody successful to cheer about. The courageous ex-Plant Works employee, a member of a family steeped in the boxing business, Bruce became British, British Empire and European heavyweight champion. But it wasn't easy. Fighters then, as today, got hurt and Bruce suffered more than most, especially against men like the Polish-American Joe Baksi in 1947. This happy family picture taken by a *Sheffield Star* photographer shows him with his wife Norah, Bruce junior, and baby Janet. Bruce eventually retired, to the licensed trade in Bolsover and Edlington, and a haulage business.

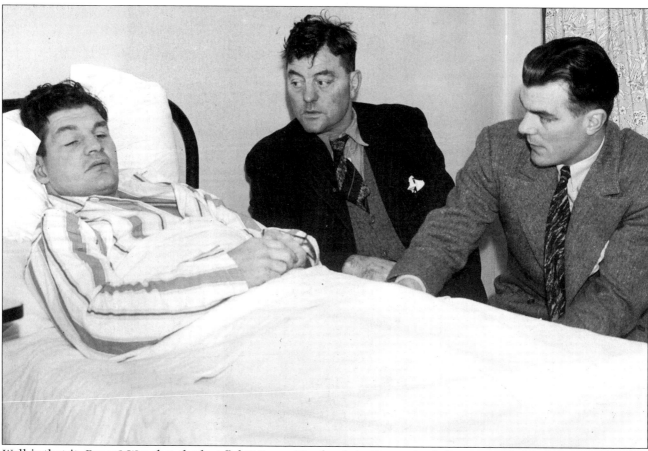

Well is that it, Bruce? Was that the last fight? Bruce Woodcock in Doncaster Infirmary with his father and brother Billy at his bedside perhaps deciding the next move.

Football:

It's Charlie... no it isn't, it's Kevin! Keegan like they would never recognise him in Newcastle, Hamburg, Liverpool and elsewhere. Doncaster has produced many fine footballers, and none better than the man who is now the boss and big spender at Newcastle and the toast of Tyneside. The son of an Armthorpe miner, Kevin first played soccer with a local team on land near Doncaster racecourse. A pupil of Roberts Road School, on Balby Bridge, it was his Roman Catholic headmistress who first spotted his talent. Given a trial by Doncaster Rovers he was told 'Come back when you're a bit bigger, lad!' but he was eventually signed by Scunthorpe – and the rest is history.

The real Charlie Chaplin, by the way, played the Doncaster theatre in his youth, and made a little publicised nostalgic visit to the town 40 years ago, staying at the Danum. Very few recognised him, and he rather enjoyed the anonymity.

Kevin Keegan again, photographed this time for a World Cup 1982 Personalities feature, playing of course for England. Keegan's League club then was Southampton. As you can see, it was the time when hair was long, and shorts were shorter.

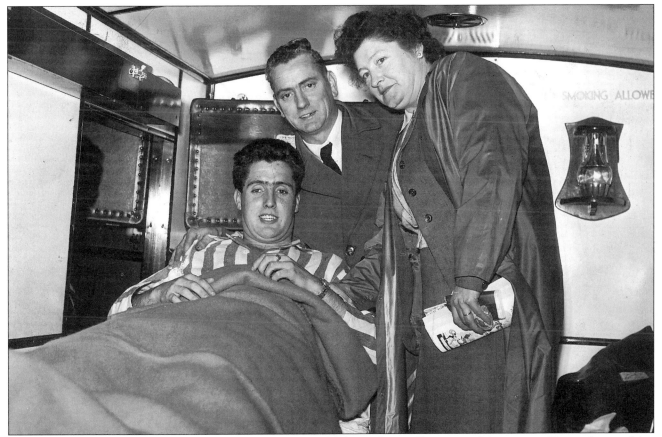

The moment every footballer dreads – a serious injury which can jeopardise a promising career. None who saw him play will ever forget Doncaster Rovers' Alick Jeffery, one of the most powerful strikers of his day, who broke a leg in an Under-23 International. He is pictured in the ambulance accompanied by his father and mother.

It's the Chas and Alick Show! The two former Doncaster Rovers stars Alick Jeffery, who became a Doncaster licensee, and Charlie Williams, much-loved star comedian ('Me owd flower' remember?).

Doncaster Rovers with Jackie Bestall manager, became Third Division Northern section champions 1946-47 and spent a year in the Second Division. They had notched 72 points, two more than Spurs' back in 1919-20. And Clarrie Jordan, formerly a miner at South Kirkby, scored 42 league goals, a club record. Some of the players in that memorable season can be seen in this picture taken in November 1949. Back row (left to right): Lowes, Hainsworth, Bycroft, Hardwick, Hodgson, Goodfellow. Front row: Tindill, Todd, Bennett, Doherty (player-manager), Calverley.

Doncaster Rovers in 1957. Back row (left to right): Makepeace, Graham, Burgin, Kilkenny, Williams (Charlie Williams, who went on to enjoy a highly successful career as a comedian), Hopkinson. Front row: Mooney, Nicholson, Tindill, Cavanagh, Walker.

Another Rovers' team picture, this time the full playing staff in the 1961-62 season. Back row (left to right): Fairhurst, Haigh, Nimmo, Broadbent, Hildreth, Wales, Cope, Marshall. Middle row: Taylor, Bratt, Wright, Garnett, Staton, Lunn, Swallow, Hinton. Front row: Lodge, Leighton, Malloy, Ballagher, Veall, with Wally Ardron, standing, the trainer.

Askern Spa football club. Years before anybody ever heard of Harrogate, they were coming to Askern to sample the waters from five wells. At the turn of the century special trains came from as far off as Manchester. You drank the waters, bathed in them, and the Hydro even had its own physician.

Askern became a resort full of hotels and lodging houses. People flocked from Doncaster at weekends – on bicycles and horse-drawn transport. Then in 1911 came the colliery, and the wells were filled in, and the landladies called it a day.

Bullcroft was the colliery at Carcroft, and here is the Amateurs soccer team for the season 1914-15. Look a bit like Newcastle United, don't they!

Doncaster Rovers, 1947-48. The best they ever fielded? Newly promoted to Division Two from Division Three North, sadly they didn't stay there. Back row, from the left, Arnold Lowes, Len Hainsworth, Ken Hardwick, Syd Bycroft, Len Graham, Syd Goodfellow. Front row Herbert Tindill, Paul Todd, Ray Harrison, Peter Doherty (player-manager), Alf Calverley. Insets: Top left Jack Hodgson, right Dave Miller. Bottom left Joe Dubois, right Harry Tomlinson.

Cricket:

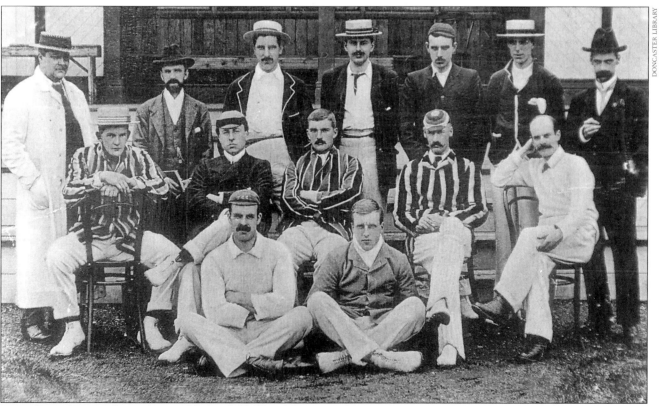

A motley mixture of gear here. This is Tickhill Cricket team in 1902.

They surely didn't play in those top hats? Or did they? Is this where they get the term 'hat trick'? This is Hatfield Cricket Club in 1900.

Basketball:

Doncaster Panthers' basketball team played Leicester City Riders in the Spring of '95. Here Panthers' Anthony 'Juice' Joseph evades Riders' George Branch.

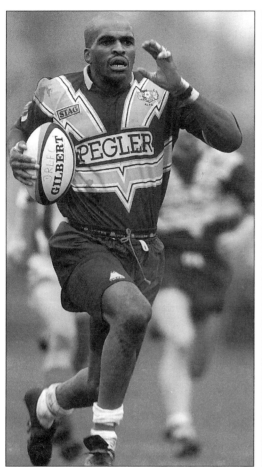

Rugby League:

All sportsmen in Doncaster followed with elation and bitter disappointment the varying fortunes of the Dons Rugby League Club since those early beginnings forty years ago. These two pictures perhaps typify their fighting spirit: Audley Pennant in full flight as he races clear and alone to score the Dons' only try against Warrington in 1994, and Wayne Jackson, ready for the bath, after the Dons' game with Salford in February 1995.

Women's Football:

Above: Doncaster Belles must be the most successful women's soccer team of all time, and our pictures show some of their memorable FA Trophy-winning moments in 1988 and 1994. In this one Karen Walker scores at Crewe and joy is unconfined. *Right:* Team manager Paul Edmunds with captain Gill Coultard and the Women's FA Trophy.

Something silver on the sideboard for everyone. Muddied but feeling marvellous, Doncaster Belles make soccer history.

Cycling:

The eighteen members of the Doncaster International Order of Good Templars Cycling Club must have been a splendid sight whizzing in formation down to Sandall Beat, in their decorated collars. All dress in similar fashion, and even the bicycles, with their carbide lamps, look to be the same model. Question: How did a Good Templar keep his or her hat on against a head wind at 15mph?

Doncaster Infirmary Harriers 1911-12. That's clear enough, but who were they? Surgeons, doctors, anaesthetists, porters, dispensers? They look hard men and we don't fancy a towelling from the fierce chap on the right. Athletics didn't loom large in the town's sporting activity at that time, but there were plenty of cricket clubs, an angling association, motor-cycling, rugby, golf, lawn tennis, and football clubs, of which Rovers Football and Athletic Club was best known. Rovers' headquarters then was in a Temperance hotel.

Schooldays

Doncaster schools were renowned for their music-making long before World War Two, teaching being done by both peripatetics and full-time staff. In those days every child could sing at least something from the National Song Book, every child longed to appear in one of those great annual concerts at the Corn Exchange, and many, as seen here at Intake, could play an instrument. This is an extraordinary picture of pioneering days but the tradition of instrumental teaching continues and can still be seen in the work of staff from the William Appleby music centre today. We leave you to imagine the sound they made.

They're 12 of the likeliest looking lads you'd ever wish to see! You were supposed to look a little solemn when you were having your photograph taken in those days; this was serious men's world stuff to be hung on the wall in the school hall.

But these boys from Intake School are just bubbling over with fun and enthusiasm. Some good players here - like Gordon Turner (centre, front), who went on to play for Luton Town in the 1959 FA Cup Final at Wembley and was also capped for England 'B'. And this is only the school second team, pictured on Townies (that's Town Fields, remember) in 1938.

INTAKE FIRST SCHOOL

Weren't they just bonny lasses!! And dear little boys ! (We'd like to think so, anyway.) Occasion was the crowning of Intake May Queen at All Saints', Intake, sometime in the 1930s. Days of innocence and days of youth ....all gone.

MISS K. BRAMWITH

Hexthorpe Infants School, 1924. Not a lot we can tell you about Hexthorpe Infants in 1924 except they could be Hexthorpe grannies and granddads today. They'd be called Doris, or Mary, or Betty or Anne. And Billy and Tommy and Arthur and John. Not a Samantha, never a Wayne or Darren among them.

Stormy Weather

"Doncaster was the warmest place in Britain yesterday." You' read that quite often, but it could also be the wettest of places. Flooding at Sprotbrough made the best pictures and here a small boat defies the torrent in 1995.

The scene at Sprotbrough, again in 1995, when canal and river merged into one great moving lake.

It's a team picture of a different sort at Belle Vue. Doncaster Rovers youth team manager Jim Golze and YTS soccer trainees in 1993. Their goal this time was a snow-free pitch.

Didn't the estate agent say 'attractive gardens front and rear'? He said nothing about a river and a lake. Heavy September rain surprised residents on the Scawsby to High Melton road in 1991.

Safe and snug, muffled and mittened, this was Ross Evans when he was 18 months old and the snow blanketed Bentley in 1991.

"If you're going down the shops bring us a small brown, large white, and a pinta please." Man with the big wellies braves the floods which marooned residents of Westminster House, Intake, in 1992.

Now look at it! We had a lovely pond here ...fish, aquatic plants, water lilies, everything. Spent a small fortune. And now look at it! Those fish'll be heading downstream to the sea wondering what's happened. When the floods subsided at Scawsby in 1991 the muddy mess beggared description.

Subscribers

1 Maurice Francis

2 J S Marshall

3 Winifred Oxenham

4 Kenneth Whitehead

5 Mr G Ellis

6 Nigel E Wright

7 Mr John Alan Dodson

8 Mr Felix Desmond Cooper
& Mrs Gwendoline Cooper

9 Norman Newcombe

10 Norman Newcombe

11 Leslie Wedgewood

12 George Reed

13 Paul Seaton

14 Brian Brough

15 Sheila Thorpe

16 Edith Easthill

17 C R Mills

18 R H Peace

19 Mrs Vera Marklew

20 Mrs Valerie Vaez-Afarani

21 R Edgley

22 Fred Holdridge

23 Michael James Elcoat

24 Mr Ted Swaby

25 Ethel Deighton

26 Brian Keefe

27 Tom & Joan Hampton
(Oliver, BC, Canada)
28 John Walker
29 Lynda Beswick
30 S W Laughton
31 Mr D W Pashley
32 Carol Whitaker
33 Enid Gilliatt
34 Martin Redmond MP
35 Gerald Selby & Margo Drury
36 Ken Drury
37 Julia Potter
38 Mary Fanthorpe
39 David Thompson
40 Ivor & Maria Procter
41 Mrs Joan Pratt
42 Roy Shaw
43 Mrs Maureen Laben
44 Mrs Dee Ashurst
45 Mr V T Dekeyser
46 Olive Sunderland
47 Nicholas J Patching
48 T A Morton
49 D N Grady
50 Mr S C A Ineson
51 Kathleen Dixon
52 Harry Edward Hoyle
53 Mr & Mrs R W Smith
54 Mr & Mrs E T Kanna
55 Mr & Mrs M W Boyfield
56 S Musson